In the Fig Tree

In the Fig Tree

❖

Surviving domestic violence in words and pictures

Edited by Grace Coleman, Amanda Denman, and John Chapin, Ph.D.

iUniverse, Inc.

New York Lincoln Shanghai

In the Fig Tree
Surviving domestic violence in words and pictures

iUniverse, Inc.

For information address:
iUniverse, Inc.
2021 Pine Lake Road, Suite 100
Lincoln, NE 68512
www.iuniverse.com

Publication was made possible through a grant from Verizon Wireless.

All proceeds from the sale of this book benefit victims of domestic violence.

ISBN: 0-595-33639-6

Printed in the United States of America

Crisis Center North is to be commended for the hope it has given to so many women in the Pittsburgh area. *"In the Fig Tree"* is yet another example of the tremendous work this organization does to raise awareness of domestic violence issues and generate support for survivors.

In 1995, when Verizon Wireless decided to devote our community service efforts to domestic violence prevention and awareness, many people asked why we chose this cause. We recognized domestic violence as an epidemic and wanted to make others aware of its affect on our society, as well. At Verizon Wireless we believe that one of the most effective ways to raise awareness of domestic violence is through open—and frequent—communication.

As a company, we openly address domestic violence in numerous ways: in our employee newsletters, on our Intranet, in our code of business conduct, and at our staff meetings. We conduct teen dating abuse sessions. We promote volunteerism by collecting school supplies and toys for children in shelters and offering employee-conducted job-skills training to their mothers. Nationwide, we have more than 1,200 Verizon Wireless store locations collecting old, no-longer-used wireless phones to be recycled for victims of domestic violence.

When Verizon Wireless decided to put communication and wireless technology to work for domestic violence victims we named our effort **HopeLine**[SM] because the name embodies the positive difference we intended to make in the areas of prevention and the life-building process.

No organization exemplifies "hope" better than Crisis Center North and that's why it is especially gratifying to be part of this unique and meaningful book project.

Roger Tang—President—Ohio/Pennsylvania Region, Verizon Wireless

I'm here. See me. No don't see me.
Notice me. No, leave me alone.
Just please love me.
Help me. Save me. Keep me safe.

~ Carol

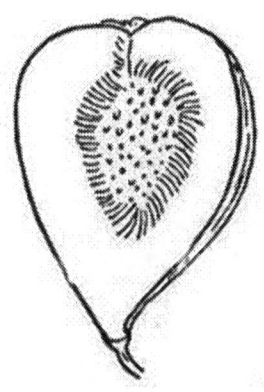

Contents

Introduction 1

    About domestic violence 1

    About this book 2

The Fig Tree 4

Words & Pictures 12

Bookshelves 13

Dream House 17

Felicity's Cat 21

Peggy's Van 24

Ship at Sea 27

Saplings 30

References 35

Domestic Violence Resources 37

ACKNOWLEDGEMENTS

Ultimately, projects without individuals to back them remain merely good ideas. This publication came to fruition because of the financial backing provided by Verizon Wireless. Thank you to Pat Quolke of Quolke Communications for unwavering belief in this and many projects sponsored by Crisis Center North and to Roger Tang and Laura Merritt of Verizon Wireless in Ohio/Pennsylvania for always listening to and supporting new ideas. Time and time again, Verizon Wireless has proven its dedication to ending domestic violence; your sponsorship of this project is yet another proof of that dedication.

This project would not have been possible without the Greater Pittsburgh Literacy Council. For over ten years, they have been sponsoring the AmeriCorps program, spreading education and hope throughout the community.

The staff of Crisis Center North supported this project while continuing their own daily programs combating domestic violence.

Special thanks to the law firm of Thorp, Reed and Armstrong for providing legal guidance throughout the parameters of this project. Ellen Milsac of Thorp, Reed and Armstrong always makes time for the staff of Crisis Center North, even in the midst of a heavy trial caseload. Ellen, thank you for believing and for protecting our good ideas. We also extend our gratitude to Jennifer Tarasi and Megan Palumbo, two attorneys whose time, patience and expertise were of the utmost importance.

Thank you to the women that participated in this workshop. We appreciate the courage and motivation it took for you to put yourselves out there. You threw yourselves wholeheartedly into this workshop, and this book is a testament to your strength. You have broken the silence that has persisted in keeping domestic violence a "private, family matter" and have shared knowledge that can only result in power.

"A thousand pens are ready to suggest what you should do and what effect you will have."

—*Virginia Woolf*

Introduction

About domestic violence...

As the last crimson and gold leaves fall from the trees, the days grow shorter and the air grows colder. It's the time of year for reflection. I'm reflecting on the many lives that have been saved this year through the efforts of our staff, volunteers, board members and benefactors. I'm also thinking about the lives that were not saved and the irrevocable void that is left in our community as a result.

Over 100 individuals needlessly lost their lives in Pennsylvania last year, because of domestic violence. On average, someone in Pennsylvania dies every three days, as a result of domestic violence. Four women in the United States are murdered each day by a male intimate partner.

It's the job of domestic violence advocates to "advocate" on behalf of domestic violence victims. It's our job to somehow help people understand the toll that violence takes both in the home and in the community at large. It's a difficult task. How do you make a community understand how a woman could be shot to death by her husband on her wedding day? How do you explain why a man attempts to cut off his wife's fingers with a meat cleaver? How do you personalize statistics to the point that people understand that each number has a face?

With the help of Verizon Wireless, we created a forum in which the voices of victims could be heard directly. We gathered; we laughed; we cried; we wrote. The result is *In the Fig Tree*. As you turn the pages of this book, what comes through are the voices of a group of survivors whom Crisis Center North has had the privilege of serving. Often, they choose not to speak of their respective victimization directly, but do so in less blatant, often more creative ways, capturing the impact that violence has had on their lives. The magic of this project was not in the end result, but in the process that each woman took to define her experience. It is a book which helped its creators understand and derive meaning from the violence that changed their lives forever, while giving readers a unique glimpse into their world. It is a book which honors the voice of the survivor and the story that she tells.

About this book...

Every little girl has dreams for her future. From prima ballerina to the WNBA, married with children or an independent world traveler, auto mechanic or homecoming queen. Over time, those dreams evolve into goals, ambitions become possibilities and choices. Like the fruit of a fig tree, they are abundant and ripe for the picking. No little girl ever dreams that she will be a victim of domestic violence. Pain, heartbreak, mistrust and insecurity are never a part of the futures that are envisioned, but it happens all too often. The same social values in the nineteen sixties that made women like Sylvia Plath believe that "choosing one meant losing all the rest" still make it possible for a man to assume the role of master, and belittle and abuse a woman into submission. Her imagination and belief in her own abilities shape each little girl's dreams. A woman's reality is shaped by the rules of patriarchal society.

"Feminist Exploration & Interpretation of Women in Violence" was a workshop designed as a safe place to openly discuss the roles of women in a patriarchal society and to better understand the system and its values. We sought to provide women with a means of positive creative self-expression, giving them back the voice that had too long been silenced. This was done through readings, discussion and writing exercises that created an ongoing dialogue to encourage empowerment.

Drawing on the perennial *Madwoman in the Attic* by Sandra M. Gilbert and Susan Gubar, we began to explore in greater detail the rich literature that our foremothers had left behind. The curriculum included the poems "The Prisoner" by Erica Jong, and "The Other Side of the Mirror" by Mary Elizabeth Coleridge; the short story of an imagination stunted and energy wasted in Charlotte Perkins Gilman's "The Yellow Wallpaper," the documentation of the cycle of violence in a brutal marriage over one hundred years before such a cycle would be recognized in Anne Bronte's *The Tenant of Wildfell Hall*; and excerpts from the female writers' manifesto, Virginia Woolf's *A Room of One's Own*. We studied their language of suffering, despair and revolt and their subversion of the system of which they were victims. We explored the ways the lives of the writers themselves were reflected in their fictional characters, thus serving as a voice for both. We looked at examples outside of literature as well, such as the lyrics of recent popular music depicting violence in relationships and the femme fatale of film noir of the nineteen forties.

At the beginning of the workshop, each woman was given a journal and encouraged to write in it whenever possible. Writing exercises included reaction pieces and reflective works. This book is the results of their efforts.

Hopefully, the experience has planted the seeds for new fig trees to blossom: that the women sharing their words and pictures with the world find their lives branching out before them, green and new. When a woman has been empowered, when she is confident in herself and is free to safely choose, the possibilities are endless in the fig tree.

The Fig Tree

○ ○

I found myself sitting in the crotch of this fig tree, starving to death, just because I couldn't make up my mind. I wanted each and every one of them, but choosing one meant losing all...

The Bell Jar is Sylvia Plath's autobiographical novel about a young woman suffering a mental breakdown. In the passage above, the narrator describes her life as a fig tree branching out before her, with each fig representing one of the different choices she faces for her future.

The women in the workshop were asked to describe their own fig trees. Had they made their choices? Could they choose more than one fig? What does this passage say about women's roles in society? Are you sitting in your fig tree right now? Does choosing one path cut off the remaining paths? Does refusing to make a choice kill all the fruit?

The following selections attempt to answer some of these questions. Some are moving accounts of the decisions made that have eventually led them to a domestic violence counseling center. More importantly, they describe the hope of getting another chance: to pluck once more from the tree of life and to taste the sweetness of an ambition fulfilled and freedom won.

~ Peggy

Way back when, I sat upon my own fig tree spying many figs of my own. They included the independence of living on my own in my own apartment, striving to achieve "officer" status in my career at one of the most prestigious financial institutions in the area, marrying and becoming a traditional wife and stay at home mother—all of which had their own specific appeal. However, being a lover of such fairytales as *Cinderella* and *Snow White*, TV shows such as the *Brady Bunch, Partridge Family* and *Leave it to Beaver*—the choice was obvious, wasn't it? It was the family life for me—the biggest, ripest fig of them all—my dream come true—the career choice of all career choices—in my mind's eye! The other figs quickly shriveled up and died and I began to partake of the "fig of choice." Being the "good," "supportive" little wife—working full time to put my husband through graduate school for the first two years of marriage—this only after having paid off his undergraduate loans for him. Then came my turn to experience my dreams and goals. With the birth of our first child, I quit working to be a stay-at-home mother—completely dependent on my husband for financial support, as well as emotional support.

Throughout the thirteen years that I stayed at home rearing my three wonderful children, I discovered much to my disappointment that my husband was not a reliable person to be dependent on. Losing each job he had and never seeing any need for personal growth or improvement on his part, either personally or professionally. The fig of our marriage withered and died, leaving me feeling mentally and emotionally beat up and taken advantage of by the very education I had paid for my husband to get. For you see, he became a social worker and then used his knowledge of mental health to mentally and emotionally manipulate me and even our children.

So there I was, thrust back upon the fig tree with new, more challenging figs before me. The new figs this time consisted of survival, career, and children. Interesting how my fig tree has never consisted of far away lands or glamorous careers. I dove into all of the figs I could gather—taking on a part-time job, in order to survive, all the while trying to keep life as normal as possible for my three children whose lives were falling apart. A large part of normal to us at this time was home-schooling. I partook of each fig to the fullest to numb the pain of the failure I felt from my failed marriage. The saddest transition was leaving my children to attain full-time status in my job and eventually work on a career. My job became the most fulfilling of the figs I had chosen this time. Letting nothing stand in my career path, I began to climb the corporate ladder at the inventory service for which I worked. I started out at entry level as an auditor counting merchandise and entering it into a small calculator-type machine. Very under confident and self conscious, lacking all self-esteem, I worked hard—not looking left or right for fear of having to interact with another human being who I was certain was much better than me. As time went on, the very person who trained me and helped build my confidence become my companion, then fiancée and husband. Something that never appeared to me on my fig tree of choices—but seemed to simply fall—like a bomb right out of the sky.

Again, I find myself in the branches of that fig tree. New figs appearing—career advancement, motherhood, traditional wife; life's lessons had changed my perspective—"achieve, achieve, achieve," "survive, survive, survive," were now my motivations. The career advancement was the fig of choice this time. Pride and self-esteem flourished, financial situation improving, missing my children, missing their important events—no support and all alone—my husband disapproving of my career advancement so much that he assaulted me because of it—he was arrested and a PFA was granted.

Back in the fig tree again! To divorce? To reconcile? Career advancement? Motherhood? Survival? Feelings of wanting some of the original "figs" of motherhood began to resurface, along with the desire for the sweetness of that career advancement fig. And of course, survival was a big one! The figs' flavors began to change—the ability to successfully choose more than one became apparent—priorities turned around again. My life appears to be like a fig tree that is forever bearing figs, new ones to pick from every day!

A nice balance of the variety of the tree seems now to be the goal. With reconciliation, motherhood, survival and career carefully blending, life is forever changing, the blend is forever changing. The balance never seems perfect—balance—the ultimate goal!

~ **Linda D.**

My fig tree is a huge tree which spans approximately 40 years. The first fig was my grandmother's desire for a share in the inheritance of her farm. Farm life is real hard work, at least to a 16 year old girl. Farming is also a way of life-not just a job. I worked hard on the farm as a teenage girl and didn't think I wanted to continue to work that hard for the rest of my life. But I still love the farm itself and the family values it represents, and I'm in the process of trying to keep my share of the inheritance.

The next fig I chose was going off to college in search of a career. College was close by—only 12 miles up the road to Penn State University. Penn State was in my blood so to speak. But the dream of becoming a college co-ed was something I wasn't totally prepared for. As a small town girl, Penn State was a huge place and very overwhelming. College became a place of self-discovery instead of a career path. This fig presented to me a chance to find the perfect husband and the chance to raise a family.

This brings me to the next fig on my tree. After much peer pressure, I fell for a Penn State Football Player. He was a big guy—somebody I felt would be strong and loving and faithful and a good provider. After all, he was a college grad. That fig turned out to be one of the most devastating and toughest lessons I ever had to learn in life. This fig fell to the ground with a thud. My husband turned out to be unfaithful, disrespectful and irresponsible.

So my next fig was a new career. Instead of wife and homemaker, I became an insurance broker. This fig represented financial independence; however, I hardly made enough money to survive in the beginning. I persevered and worked very hard—actually I worked for a solid 26 years. The first 10 years were OK, but the last 16 were arduous and I just existed—not really enjoying what I was doing anymore, but I still had to make a living for myself since I was alone.

When the next fig came along (my husband of five years now), I felt I had finally found unconditional love. After all, he told me many, many times he always wanted me to feel loved, he would always be there for me and he would always love me. On May 19, 1999, I chose this fig for better or worse, for richer or poorer. I got the worse and the poorer and I also got verbal, emotional and physical abuse. On April 10, 2003, this fig dried up and fell to the ground with a loud thud. Today is my 5th wedding anniversary and I'm spending it in a creative writing class.

The last fig on my tree represents mature independence, a sense of accomplishment and peace of mind. Although I didn't get the college degree I started out to get as a teenager, I did get it several years ago. I've had a new job for 10 months now and feel pretty good about it. I also have peace of mind that I gave my marriage 110%. Although the other figs have wrinkled and fell to the ground, those figs will never destroy my spirit. The last fig represents my life right now and with desire, determination and drive, nothing I go after will be impossible to achieve.

~ Felicity Towne

My fig tree is in flux. It blooms, remains dormant, then blooms again—a rhythm uniquely its own—never conforming to traditional seasons.

The fist petite figs were that of a school teacher and librarian. I suppose those reflected my love of school, in particular, the library. I gladly chose to volunteer my recess time in the library. Sure, I played kickball and Chinese jump rope with classmates, but loved my books and found quiet solitude far more intriguing than the alternative. As my fig tree matured, the lush figs emerged; the museum curator, the photo journalist and the psychologist. Perhaps I didn't select just one of the three figs, although I feel my life and my life's work reflect the essence of the three. I have always loved art in its many forms. Whether it's music, theater, photography, architecture, poetry or painting, I appreciate and savor art. My interest in human development, human emotions and life experiences, coupled with a deep desire to engage in socially relevant activity explains my current profession. I am a psychiatric social worker.

There was once a fig that contained every country in the world. I once said I wanted to travel to every country. A more realistic one has replaced that fig. Instead of the "travel everywhere" fig, it's simply the "travel" fig. Most recently, it assumed the shape of England. The travel fig allows me to be more open to my craving all the time.

As for another craving—there's the sensual, desirable and amazing lover fig. This fig's flavor resembles a good merlot that becomes more lush and intoxicating with age.

So the figs thus far have been ones that I've tasted or confidently squashed. There remains a small cluster that I've yet to identify. I think one is a wife fig and another a mother fig—but—I can't be certain. I know that I've had strong maternal feelings since I was quite young, and I so love being in an intimate relationship with a man I crave, adore, trust and respect, but these figs seem out of reach right now. The branches have leaned toward me on a few occasions, only to snap back in a wicked jerk…These are by far the most bittersweet figs. There's an ache inside me that lingers. I also recognize that if I choose the wrong one or I choose one before it has matured, I could very well end up with a bellyache, or worse. So, I remain patient and embrace what is in my life, rather than what is lacking.

~ **Carol**

It's sad that I didn't even realize I had a choice. I just thought life happened. I was raised to believe there were two gods. The one in Heaven that I was brainwashed by the nuns to believe that if I wasn't the perfect Catholic girl, I would go straight to Hell…or maybe, if I was just a little bad, I would stop off at Purgatory for a couple of lifetimes to pay for my sins. And when God, in his infinite wisdom, would let me arise—glide through the perpetual gates of white billowing clouds and purity—I would go to Heaven. If you think I am highly pissed at what I was taught, harassed and scared into believing. You're right.

Or the other god: A physically, emotionally and sexually abusive alcoholic father. But I don't believe the alcohol had a thing to do with it. It just served as his excuse. He was just cruel.

I think about what I could have become with a little, just a little, love, kindness and support. It hurts at times; I feel extremely angry. Anger is an emotion I wasn't allowed to show or even feel, because that, too, was a sin—with both holy fathers.

Despite all this, I'm so glad that I became aware that I do have choices. I didn't even know I had a "fig tree." This is about becoming aware, because I was so controlled. I realize I didn't fully understand what having choice meant; that I can choose, I can make a mistake, and it's OK. I can choose again.

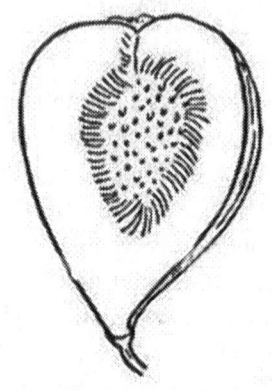

Words & Pictures

What does this picture make you think of?

Ask a thousand different people that question and you are bound to receive a thousand different answers. An image can have a powerful impact on a person's imagination. It can conjure up memories, emotions, thoughts and experiences.

Each week, one woman shared a photograph of an object or image that for her had a special meaning. After studying the photograph, each woman had 15 minutes to write their own interpretation of the image. Many of the women had not written very much and were self-conscious about the quality of their work. By placing time restrictions, the women were less inclined to inhibit their thoughts.

A picture really is worth a thousand words. The following capture unique glimpses of survivors. Her words. Her pictures.

Bookshelves

~ Peggy

I feel a sense of curiosity, a desire to look at each book's title and possibly read a few passages from a title that interests me.

I am reminded of the simple dates my husband and I share at the local bookstores. On occasion we will get a nice warm cup of coffee, tea or cider at the bookstore and then peruse the shelves of books together. When we find a book that interests one of us, we read portions aloud to each other—sharing many things from educational material to humorous, to poetic, to spiritual works.

We normally find ourselves sprawled out on the floor in front of one of the bookcases enjoying our own quiet time together—barely noticing that there are any other shoppers around. Although we typically have no specific book in mind to purchase, we will ultimately leave with a new treasure to take home and share.

I find this environment quite warm, relaxing and romantic. My husband and I have discovered many wonderful things about each other through our trips to the bookstore. Our reading together has provoked many interesting and enlightening conversations.

~ Felicity Towne

Crowded shelves. I think of my own bookshelves, not so crowded. The photo reminds me of those tucked away sections of the library or a great used bookstore where the scent of aged paper and cloth-bound hard covers take me back. Back where? I'm not quite sure.

I've always loved libraries and used bookstores—Quiet places with so much history and adventure. I would spend hours there. A dropped book, a burst of laughter—something would always pique my interest and challenge that taboo of noise...

There's something very exciting about walking around places like that. I love sitting in a cozy chair or on the floor, reading at my leisure, whatever and how much I want to throw in. A roaming Bathsheba dog or a few interested or not so interested glances from a stranger, and you've set the mood. Good grief, where is this going?

Oh, right, crowded shelves. Every once in a while I like to browse over the books I've read...

~ Linda D

A shelf of books like those in Mandy's picture reminds me of my basement at home, because my husband collects and sells used and antiquarian books as a hobby, and for the past two and a half years for his income. Although I initially liked the idea of having him collect books, now that he has not been working for such a long time, I feel they are sustaining him financially just enough so that he does not have to take responsibility to actively find employment. Because the books have provided him with some income, he lacks the ambition and drive to find gainful employment. I have gotten to the point of where the books are taking up too much room in the house and have been "in the way," which also prevents him from doing home remodeling in the basement. The books he sells mostly on e-bay, which ties up the computer and phone line for hours and hours. Before I returned to work last August, people said they couldn't get me by phone because the phone line was always busy, and it was because he was always on e-bay selling his books.

The picture reminded me of my house and also that I have my own personal books which I would like to display on shelves but cannot do so, since there is no more room in the house for my books.

Dream House

~ Mandy

Welcome to Suburbia

The Cunninghams

Wally and the Beave

All of life's problems

Resolved in half an hour

Kids playing outside

Mom in the garden

But what do these walls hide?

This is not a set

This is not Lot 15

In sunny Burbank California

This is someone's home

These are someone's walls and windows

And the blinds go down

And the kids go inside

And a half an hour can't resolve

What's for dinner?

Let alone the deeper questions

of our brief existence.

Walk through that trellis

And you're walking into someone's world

"Let's have a return to family values"

"Let's have a return to the unbreakable bond

of the American nuclear family"

Let's stop kidding ourselves

A well-kept garden does not a happy family make.

And a mom and a dad and two kids in the yard

(or is it cats)

Either way, Mr. Crosby, Mr. Nash

Life might still be hard.

But this is a very fine house

In all of its back-from-the-road-

But-close-to-the-neighbors-hotdogs-catch-in-the-backyard-flower-growing-cookie cutter

Innocence and passivity

This is the house that Jack built

And I know Jack, he's a decent guy.

But this isn't the house that Jack lives in

Someone else's family is in there

A regular Mr. and Mrs. C

'Cept Mrs. C's not allowed beyond the trellis

And Mr. C is no Tom Bosley

And this house

Despite all outward appearances

Just isn't a HOME.

~ *Peggy*

Beautiful, colorful, clean and bright. Peaceful and calm. Sweet smelling fragrance of flowers. The perfect atmosphere for a relaxing afternoon spent alone lying in the cool grass, reading a good book. Breaking from the reading to watch butterflies and birds, to listen to the chirping of the birds, the buzzing of the bees and to feel the gentle breeze of the warm summer air.

The perfect surroundings to pray in Thanksgiving, for all of the beauty and goodness in the world. Being close to nature in this way causes me to ponder the miracle of it all—how the flowers grow, how the bees pollinate, how the sun and rain play a part—such a magnificent creation all there just for me to enjoy! The wonder of it all!

What a glorious break from the day to day stresses, chores and responsibilities. Such a contrast to the hustle and bustle of everyday living. Such an opportunity to stop and smell the roses.

Felicity's Cat

~ Felicity Towne

OK, so some people talk about their children—I talk about my cat. This is Meya. She's four years old and she came to live with me when she was seven weeks old. I live alone with Meya; my family lives four hours east of Pittsburgh. Months pass and my only source of affection is in the form of kitty cuddling. She greets me at the door at the end of the day, she sits along the edge of the tub when I take a bath, and when I lounge on my deck, she sits at the window, crying to join me outside. When I exercise and meditate, she struts about, tail flicking to and fro—just enough distraction to throw me off course. And lastly, she sleeps in my bed. Oh, to be so loved!

So perhaps she's just a cat—but she's a very cool cat who has been through it with me. Meya is the only witness to the multiple assaults against me. One dreaded 26 hour period of time in particular—she hid in the far reaches of my closet inside a duffel bag, under clothes. I had to search for her after he left. I can only imagine how freaked out the little dear must have felt. She was with me that night I thought I might be killed…these are just words on paper now…they fail to reflect the chaos, the shock, the…

So she's my Meya. She makes my house feel like a home.

~ Linda

A relaxing afternoon, lying in the sun. The warmth of the rays upon your skin. The sun upon your back, making tension burn away. No need to hide your breath. Just to breathe so naturally, taking in the air that you forgot existed. To stretch as though your body had added length without end.

No one's fingers in your ribs. No one's hand holding you back. No one's insults you can hear. No one's eyes watching over you. The freedom that a cat can feel and what each of us can only look for within ourselves. And wishing that a warm windowsill would a little larger, so that there would be room enough for me.

Peggy's Van

~ **Anonymous**

White, pristine, mobile, contained,

The perfect image of the modern day mother.

Reliable, dependable, capable of carrying heavy loads and noisy children.

The perfect image of the modern day mother.

Rolling on smoothly from the elementary school, to the orthodontist or to soccer practice.

The perfect image of the modern day mother.

Plant dirt, dog hair, spilled ice cream infiltrate the fibers of my upholstery—the "not so perfect image of the modern day mother.

Only when you look inside can you see that I am more than the perfect image of the modern day mother.

I am the glue that holds together the threads of my hectic family life.

The invisible force that binds our lives together.

~ Mandy

I used to collect hot wheels as a little girl. I had zillions of them. I also had a tool-box (toy of course) that I would use to be a mechanic. We had this high couch and me and my koala bear Joe would slide under it on our backs with the toolbox and "fix the car." I had a race-track too.—Well, if I'm being honest, I still do. I collect toys in general but cars in particular: hot wheels, remote control. It's funny because there is no doubt that I have always been a girly-girl. But something in me, from a very young age, rebelled against that—or more importantly, against what that's supposed to mean.

Going back to my current toy collection, I can honestly say that the majority of them are what would be considered "boy toys." Besides hot wheels and plastic tools, I didn't really have any other masculine hobbies as a young girl. So it's like now, I'm making up for lost time. Damn it, if I couldn't play with them then, well I'm certainly going to now. My boy toys extend from the cars and plastic tool belt to include pirate swords, light sabers, and transformers; even little green army men, some of whom I melted in the sun—complete with ketchup for gore. I did that in 10th grade. I guess it's just been my way of re-examining and re-defining what it means to be a "girly-girl." Collecting and playing with the toys that boys play with, now as an adult, is a kind of regressive therapy, I guess. And it sure is a hell of a lot of fun. I'm a big girl now: my clothes can get dirty; my nails can get broken; and I still feel confident in my femininity. We girls can do anything—like Barbie—or like Ken.

Ship at Sea

~ **Anonymous**

Stranded on an island, lying like a beached whale on my side. All that is missing are my struggling attempts at breath. Unable to move...motionless, alone, unsure if the waters will ever again splash against my sides. Stranded. Unable to even imagine that any direction will be possible to me again. Stranded. Unnoticed. I wonder if those who wander by even for a moment take the time to reflect on my journey. Do they wonder about the storm that hurled me toward the shore? Do they intellectualize my crash, or do they feel my pain? Do they blame me for the uncontrollable force of the wind and the waves? Do they believe I am to blame? I feel their accusations. How can they judge when they have never journeyed from the shore? Do they recognize I am alive? Do they see that I have survived?

~ Peggy

The boat had sailed too long ago.
The wind was gone.

The boat resting on a beach alone. It seems to have been beached sideways getting close to the shore. Running out of water.

Just waiting for the ocean or lake to reach up and meet it and when it does it will move again to be freed from the sand and grit. The soft water will give support and hold it up off the side that it rests upon being straightened and erect in the water. The mast with the flag of ownership.

Somewhere your heart the mast seems to have been looking for, the water your soul to help you stand alone.

~ LeAnn

The past several years, I get images of where I am in life. When the divorce began, I felt like a ship that had just discovered a serious crack and survival would be intense. There would be rough seas ahead and direction would be provided through faith and hope.

As the last year has unfolded, my most recent image has been of a boat just ship-wrecked. Finally, weathered the rough seas, and landed. Landed and made it. Still alive. Still grounded, centered and with a newly developed character that has been chiseled at like a fine piece thru the opportunity of trials and tribulations.

It is a new land, one that my moccasins have not traveled. Thank God, the storm has lifted. Its darkness finally lifted. A new place waits to be discovered. I am excited to go forward and learn and continue on this new path of my journey. It is good to be alive and continue on this new path of my journey. It is good to be alive and looking forward to life again.

Saplings

~ Linda

I wrote this September 8, 2001, almost one year after I broke his and my heart at the same time. It is a horrible sound to be able to hear two hearts breaking at the same time. It is worse when you break a heart with their lies and my own bad eyesight. We were standing in a guest room at someone else's home. I was going to send this to him; but I feared he would have another heart attack. It just took too long to break his heart.

Lied memories of Jerry.

All of these would remain as is pink roses.
Your hair and skin without the lies.
How truly different two lives could have been.

The blue and green upon their walls always would be seen through their eyes.
Never knowing the hold of lied dreams.

The pictures just two out of place small faces held within.
How the small eyes cried when they realized how different a life could have been.

Decorating someone else's Christmas tree.
A life sorely missed.
Too many apologies never made.
Too many New Year's never kissed.
Too many missed birthday candles, hot dogs and rainy Wednesday afternoons.
Too many times missed.
Re-falling in love on the first day of summer.
Three decades had passed too soon.

Never to see the young girls in their pale pink dresses or hold their hands or touch their hair with soft caresses.

The lies had taken the dreams away.
The damage had been done.
The hurt so deep we couldn't cry as one.

And as we sit with others between us, just to remember our faces in the sun;
And to realize without the lies what wonders our lives could have done.

~ Carol

Being a victim of abuse is like being convicted and serving time for a crime you didn't commit. The years lost. Friends, happiness, peace: I can't help but think about what I could have done and become with just a little support, kindness and love. Fear has truly ruled my life. But with the support of others and knowledge, I know that I don't have to be a prisoner of fear. I have the right to be free.

~ Linda

March Madness is what they called it.
That night I can still see as a colored photograph in my mind. One remains. Too permanently.

Perhaps it was the heat or the chill of the game. Or just my bad eyesight. And to this day, the unintentional pain still remains. Because of your March Madness with me.

The children you used: the ones that called you friend. You used children to pass along your threat, and then it was my choice. A man like you. A coward, was my thought.

March Madness is what they called it.

I was 15. You were 28. Was it the anger of rejection or embarrassment that would make you hide behind those children with twin eyes and a badge?

Was the injection of a VD infection to seal a broken heart—yours?

March Madness is what they called it.

A confession to my family would not hold the truth. And now you hide behind them and your March Madness with me.

And years pass and days go by and still with your lies that you cannot look into my eyes and not see what your madness has done to me.

References

Blaser, John. "No Place for a Woman: The Family in Film Noir and Other Essays." URL: http://www.lib.berkeley.edu/MRC/noir/index.html (June 2002).

Braddon, Mary Elizabeth. *Lady Audley's Secret*. Oxford: Oxford University Press, 1998.

Bronte, Anne. *The Tenant of Wildfell Hall*. Oxford: Oxford University Press, 1998.

Bronte, Charlotte. *Jane Eyre*. New York: Penguin Classics, 1996.

Coleridge, Mary Elizabeth. "The Other Side of a Mirror." URL: http://people.bu.edu/tgoss/anthology/poets/COLERIDGEnf.html (2003).

Gilbert, Sandra M., Gubar, Susan. *The Madwoman in the Attic: The Woman Writer and the Nineteenth Century Literary Imagination*. New Haven: Yale University Press, 2000.

Gilman, Charlotte Perkins. "The Yellow Wallpaper." URL: http://etext.lib.virginia.edu (2004).

Jong, Erica. "The Prisoner." URL: http://www.ericajong.com/poems/theprisoner.htm (1997-2002)

Mills, Michael. "High Heels on Wet Pavement." URL: http://www.moderntimes.com/palace/film_noir/index.html (1999).

Muller, Eddie. *Dark City: The Lost World of Film Noir*. New York: St. Martin's Griffin, 1998.

Muller, Eddie. *Dark City Dames: The Wicked Women of Film Noir*. New York: Harper Collins, 2001.

Plath, Sylvia. *The Bell Jar.* New York: Harper and Row, 1971.

Woolf, Virginia. *A Room of One's Own.* San Diego: Harcourt, Inc., 1989.

Domestic Violence Resources

Crisis Center North is a counseling facility whose mission is to serve victims of domestic violence and to eliminate the community held beliefs and behaviors which perpetuate it. All of Crisis Center North's services are free and confidential. If you live in the northern areas of Allegheny County, PA and you need help, please call our 24-Hour Hotline: (412) 364-5556.

Pennsylvania Coalition Against Domestic Violence: 800-932-4632
www.pcadv.org

National Domestic Violence Hotline: 1-800-799-SAFE (7233)

National Sexual Assault Hotline: 1-800-656-HOPE (4673)
www.rainn.org

All proceeds from the sale of this book go directly to Crisis Center North to fund free counseling, legal advocacy, medical advocacy and violence prevention education.

0-595-33639-6

www.ingramcontent.com/pod-product-compliance
Lightning Source LLC
Chambersburg PA
CBHW061223280526
45784CB00006B/2610